Gaps and Verges

UNIVERSITY OF CENTRAL FLORIDA PRESS

ORLANDO

Contemporary Poetry Series

Cover photograph by Jean N. Locey

Gaps
and
Verges

POEMS BY

Roald Hoffmann

Library of Congress Cataloging-in-Publication Data

Hoffmann, Roald.
    Gaps and verges: poems / by Roald Hoffmann.
        p.   cm. — (University of Central Florida contemporary poetry series)
    ISBN 0-8130-0943-X (alk. paper)
    I. Title.   II. Series.
PS3558.O3468G3   1990
811'.54—dc20   89-30487
                    CIP

University Presses of Florida is the central agency for scholarly publishing of the State of Florida's university system, producing books selected for publication by the faculty editorial committees of Florida's nine public universities. Orders for books published by all member presses should be addressed to University Presses of Florida, 15 NW 15th Street, Gainesville, Florida 32603.

Acknowledgments

I am grateful to the editors of the following magazines, in which some of the poems in this volume appeared: *Southwest Review* ("Evolution"); *thirteen* ("Intuition," "Height," "Hydropathic"); *Prairie Schooner* ("Hitchhiking," "June 1944"); *The New York Quarterly* ("Svoloch"); *Negative Capability* ("Stretch Marks"); *Piedmont Literary Review* ("Christmas, or Was It a Birthday"); *The Journal* ("Modes of Representation"); *kentucky poetry review* ("Organic, Inorganic"); *Nimrod* ("In Need of Mending"); *Hampden-Sydney Poetry Review* ("Eschatology," under a different title); *Triquarterly* ("Grand Unification"); *Alabama Literary Review* ("The Man for Whom Everything Came Easy," "Terrorists"); *The Laurel Review* ("Carcinoma"); *South Coast Poetry Journal* ("Corral"); *Folio* ("Be Wanting"); *The Jacaranda Review* ("What We Have Learned about the Pineal").

I owe a special debt to Kathleen Gemmell for her comments on this manuscript, to Jean Locey for the cover art, and to Ed Dobb for his help with "Jerry-Built Forever." A. R. Ammons, David Burak, and Phyllis Janowitz continued to give their valuable criticism and support. A number of the poems in this volume were written during a residency at an inspiring place, the Djerassi Foundation.

for Eva

Contents

One

Evolution

I had written three pages
on how insects are such good chemists, citing
the silkworm sex attractant,
and the bombardier beetle,
spraying out hot hydrogen peroxide when threatened.
And I was in the middle
of telling the story of the western pine beetle,
which has an aggregation pheromone
calling all comers (of that species).
The pheromone has three components:
one from the male, frontalin,
exo-brevicomin wafted by the female
and (ingenious)
abundant, pitch-smelling myrcene
from the host pine.
I had written this the night before,
broken it down into short lines.
When I woke up Sunday and sat down to work,
quietly, with a second cup of coffee,
the sun was on my desk.
I had some flowers I had picked on the hill
in a vase: bush lupine, California poppies,
and some of the grass that grows here.
On the grass stalks the bracts were a few centimeters apart.
They were beige, finely lined husks,
their line set by a dark spikelet,
more like a stiffened flagellum than a thorn.
A hint of something feathered inside.
The sun's warmth had burst some of the pods,
which had fallen on the draft
(the words were lost in the sun), fallen
by chance next to the shadows of seed still hanging, and,
the grass seed,
like dormant grasshoppers,
legs of now bent spikelets
cast second, finer shadows.
Then I saw you walking on the hill.

3

Intuition

The red-haired woman
said glass
is tense.
She didn't know
about disordered
silica chains, rings
and structural
frustration.
She just looked
at its fractured
green
edge.

Intravenous

It
itself
not wet, the white
redbud's broad leaf
offers strong rain
halt,
a bounce,
an inclined run, mingling
of little waters, birthing
droplets at this near perfect
heart's edges.
Tiny burdens, a memory
of Christmas tree globes, can't
be borne
indefinitely.
A great, green
heart, freed, jumps,
showing its gray bottom,
startling
droplets still
left,
into fall,
off, to the puddle
where the tree trunk sinks,
where the heart of the tree drinks.

Hitchhiking

I counted thirty-eight
red, yellow and green
helium balloons

someone had tied to
a string. The string
was bound to a stake:

the balloons whipped
around, the free end
again and again

forgetting the tether.
I went to the stake
and lay with my head

next to it, so that I
could sight along the
fluttering line. That

way the sky shrunk.
The balloons hid one
another, so I couldn't

count them again, but
I saw the one at the end
was green. I pulled

the string back to feel
the lifting force.
The sky burned blue.

I pumped the line
to see if wave motion
could be set up, if

it could be concentrated
so that the snap at the
end could set one free.

Human, All-Too-Human

they are, those fuzzy little balls
curled into the right fork in the gum.
Nearer, resolving into black eye
patches, leathery nose, a hanging
loose of arms to scratch the way we
just know a teddy bear or Pooh does
scratch. Even the pouch is sewed on
backwards. So comfy a hug, a fit.

Cousin Leo, whose mother died young,
once held a nurse. Oh, she looks so
good in white, he said, my Magyar
Florence Nightingale. He didn't let
her change her clothes at night.
The nurse grew tired of Leo (who
wasn't much good at earning a living
in Szeged or Australia) and because
it was not a time for divorce, she
gave him hell after dark, beat the kids.

So you can't tell about koalas either.
Sweetness and light, fluffy ears?
Up close, there are scars to show
that strong clawing is what makes
this niche fit. The young are weaned
on a thin eucalypt soup lapped off
the mother's anus; even before, blind,
grub-like, many don't make the un-
aided climb to that cute pouch.

Svoloch

This one's for you, sallow third man
in the row of customs officials at
Sheremetovo. Marina Tsvetaeva, in Paris,

would have loved the quiet voice
in which you pointed out that some of her
twenties' poems in this four-volume

New York edition were disrespectful
to Soviet authority. To you, she would
have thrown a quizzical smile from

under her bangs, and with a stylish wave
of her hand, she would have said "Oh
well—it's good, my friend, to see

someone reads my verses." After all,
you know so much more about Russian
literature than the freckled young

soldier, the first line of protection
of the Soviet borders, who, having spotted
one Russian book in my suitcase, called

for his still uniformed but beefier
superior, who in turn found (not that they
were hidden) three novels by Aksyonov.

But for you, the expert in a gray suit,
authority, it was left to take Tsvetaeva,
two slim volumes of Joseph Brodsky, and,

68 years after the Great October
Revolution, in the consummate act
of defense of the motherland, to confiscate

the cassette of the Haydn cello
concertos, played by Mstislav
Rostropovich, such sweet subversion.

Some Mornings Everything Goes Right

Stepping out of the bathroom
I toss the opened Klee's Pedagogical Sketchbook I was reading
to my bed.
So that I can wash my hands.
Usually my aim is bad.
But here is action: the book flips, closing,
opening,
this yellow squarish bat,
like Larry Bird's 3-pointer, long
in flying,
like a solid, closing to a plane, to a line
at one point in its trajectory,
trading momentum,
compactifying
to a perfect landing, title up
on my unmade bed's pillow.

Real

For Olof Lagercrantz

Seamounts
just below the surface,
they seem to be. One night
you were swimming with strong strokes
and they cut you,
the salt stung but you kept on,
not wanting to show you were afraid
of what's under
water.

Asking
quietly around,
you find their presence
doubted. No one else has seen them,
they say, it's just a deep sea,
no angelfish or coral,
so deep.

You return
in the early morning hours
when you can't sleep, you're alone
and you swim around, try to define them
without touching.
You remember
how they cut; you think
you know where they are.

You come back
again, carrying sacks
of words (which is all you have),
build cofferdams and caissons, encapsulating
what's down there; it will
be revealed.
Words tumble into place,

pleasuring others. Here they build
a papier-mâché mold, there, the construction
is airy-strong and supple
like a spider's framework silk.
Words craft textures
round the shapes
underneath:
you hear
their sense
in the worlds
in your mind.

One day
it is time
the others see.
So you bring them by, tell them
of the wine-dark sea and what cuts
underneath—you show them the sluices, the storm
you've diverted
into a glass
box.

It's a success,
a good party. One
likes the sheen of the silk curtain,
another admires the caisson airlock
and wants to license it. Someone remembers
how he also was afraid
of swimming in the dark,
how he once brushed
against
an eel.

They laugh
and cry. Some
even stay to see you
break the gates, strip the curtains,
open all the structures to see
nothing there—the sea

as it was
as it will be—the sea
and around you the words rise, only words,
entwined, composing
a trellis on an ark,
gulls diving for jellyfish.

Two

June 1944

The woman leads her brothers across a ditch. They
lean on her, their muscles too weak
for walking after fifteen months
hiding in an attic.

Rain mired the Russian tanks near Berezhany,
and the Ukrainian who hid them said
they must walk, across the soaked
fields of early summer,

away from the house, the attic. German troops
were still in the village, and neighbors
said they smelled Jews
hiding. So one night

they bound rags around their shoes and set out
toward the Russian lines. The woman
was tired, but when the boy,
six, couldn't walk

(did he cry?) she lifted him on her back. The wind
was new to the boy. In the attic one brick,
end-on, was out of the wall.
He watched children

play outside through this rectangular mask.
The children looked flat, and had a habit
of jumping out of view. Their giggles
bounced in, but no wind,

for the brick hole was small. Parts of the attic
the boy wasn't allowed to be in (the boards
might creak). Dried peas in a sack
made a good pillow.

So it was right for the boy to reach to the wind
to hug it, but the big guns then took
the wind from him, his mother
stumbled, he had to grab

her coat. The hedge swung off up the hill, and
they had to cross the field, the brother
who had been with the partisans
said. He had the gun

with four bullets (but there were five of them). So
they moved slowly, feet sinking into clay,
exposed, as they were, to the road,
dawn, to the Russian lines.

2

Tanks (thank God for the red star) rutted
the road, made them jump back. We are Jews,
they called up to the trucks, we want to go
to Złoczów. One stopped, Russian soldiers

climbed slowly over the side, some wrapped
in blankets, smelling of vodka and cabbage.
They gave the men handrolled cigarettes,
the boy a hard candy. One said to his mother

in Yiddish, I'm from Odessa, and pulling
out a worn book, look, I have my Peretz
with me. The soldiers hugged themselves, coats
flapping, pissed by the road and told them they

could climb up and ride as far as they went.
The others slept, but the boy looked over
the side of the truck as it lurched around
craters, stopping to let tanks pass. He saw a leg

in a ditch, then a body crooked in the way of
dead things, and he thought: that must be a German.

He saw trucks with Katyushas, crews cleaning
the tube racks, stacking shells. He imagined

them fired at night. Another body, two
arms, a helmet. No blood in this mud, just
soldiers cursing a flat tire in Russian under
gray skies. His mother called him and he came.

3

The Russian truck left
them five kilometers from the town.
They bought some milk, bread, kielbasa from a farmer
who gave them a look, but took the gold

coin. The boy swallowed
the milk, didn't like it, he had
not drunk any for three years. They slept in a barn, walked
into town the next morning. A Polish woman

sweeping her gateway
recognized them. She frowned
Ah the Rosen family, so they didn't kill you all.
Their house was standing, the biggest

house on Jagiellonska.
Only the roof was shot up.
When they knocked, a man came to the door: We live here
we thought you . . . wouldn't be back. The furniture

was gone, but the stamped
enameled tile ovens stood in the corner
of each room. In the attic they looked for the pictures
they had hidden. The boy found his mother

crying, baby pictures
(is that me, is that me?) around her.
Photos of a man pushing a baby carriage in a sunny park,
a man holding hands with his mother.

Believing

When I was eight I was a Catholic
for a while. In 1946, Kraków, it was
time to start school, and only

the parochial ones were working.
So my parents said we had converted
during the war. That got me in.

My best grades were in Catechism.
I wasn't Catholic, but I wasn't
sure what I was. In church I

carried a censer and had my first
communion in white shorts. The priest
taught us to swallow the Host. You

weren't supposed to chew it, even
if it felt as if you would gag.
The sisters gave us colored pictures

of saints if we did well in class.
I remember confession, boys shoving
to get the soft priest. Sometimes

you didn't know who was in the
confessional. You had to sift your
sins; the priest wanted not just

a lie, but something like stealing
a soccer ball or looking at your
mother in the bath. He would ask:

How many times? Then you could get
away with a scolding and three quickly
said Hail Mary's. You wouldn't want

to confess really dark things, like
looking with the janitor's son at
his younger sister's sex, poking

her with a fork. The priest would be
angry, and who knows what the gilded
black woman on the altar, the one

I didn't believe in, but who looked
at me as I walked in my white robe behind
the priest, who knows what she might do.

Two Fathers

I suppose my stepfather was a good man. It's not
that I didn't like him, he just wasn't my father,
who was a hero. I don't really remember my father.
In photographs there is a man pushing a baby carriage,

a man holding up a laughing child dressed up in
a Carpathian costume. I heard stories from my mother
of how he was hazed as a Jew at Lwów Polytechnic,
I've seen him in Zionist youth group photos

with my mother. I read the notes he made in the camp
on a book on relativity theory, and I've heard
(again from my mother) how they went to Brody,
his first job as a civil engineer being to build

a cobblestoned street there, and how they stayed
in the house of the local priest. My mother sometimes
told these stories with my stepfather there. The war
came, we were in a ghetto, a labor camp, then toward

the end my mother and I were hidden by a Ukrainian
schoolteacher. My father was killed in an attempt
to organize a mass breakout from the camp. I was five
when the news came to us in the Ukrainian's attic,

and I cried, because my mother cried. That's when
my father became a hero, which he was. The war
ended, 80 of 12,000 Jews in our town survived.
In Kraków, where we went in 1945, my mother met

my stepfather, who had lost his wife in the war,
and they married. I was eight, and though my stepfather
tried and took me on carousels, I didn't want him.
Later I built up a theory that my mother remarried

to provide me with a father, not because she liked him.
But friends who knew them say they were in love.
In the U.S. my stepfather didn't try—he was busy
working, first in a luncheonette on Delancey Street,

and when that failed, as a bookkeeper. When he
was angry he raved in his room, then sulked long.
We never made up in our family. Any punishment
(I was too good a child for that) was left to my mother.

My father was talked about all the time, and that
is how my sister, born in Queens, found out she
and I had different fathers. When my stepfather
and I had a fight about my getting married

to a girl who wasn't Jewish (I think he was hurt
by this more than my mother) I told him
he wasn't my father. He died in 1981, and
when I get angry I see that I sulk like him.

Three

Jerry-Built Forever

1

We think that all that matters
can't be deep, but chunk-to-
knowledge-chunk in subsurface
veins, and we, mind-armed miners

search/dance to lift earth cover,
free the plan. The world, oh it
waits patiently to be known,
and we do know much: what

the bombardier beetle sprays;
the salts, silts and organics,
the gradients in the Azov
sea; far bangs and dodges

of light in space; how vitamin
B_{12} twists one pyrrole ring
as it is made. Terra incog-
nita shrunk to the way the birch

bark peels and why he dressed
in white the night he sealed
the garage door cracks and
turned on the engine . . .

2

This biconcave bialy platelet
of the erythrocyte, the red
heart of the blood, holds the oxygen
carrier, hemoglobin. Four coiled

polypeptide chains, four subunits
changing pairwise twice in the fetus

to let it soak up placental O_2
steadily. Each chain a globular

protein, juxtaposed twining
of helical segments, predestined
kinks, sequences of amino acids
alike in sperm whale and horse,

a meander of bonds around
the flat disc that colors all . . . heme,
the active site, the oxygen binding
site, a porphyrin, iron. Oxygen,

enflamer, winds to a pocket
molded by protein, binds iron, moves
it in consummation, chains
tethering heme tense—a far

subunit feels the first heme's bond
quiver, the chains pull, O_2 binds
easier. Cooperativity, an allosteric
protein. In 1937

not long before the war,
Felix Haurowitz watched crystals
of deoxyhemoglobin
shatter on oxygenation.

3

Beauty whirls rococo
in fussy chains round
the oxygen pocket; beauty
cambers simple—the iron

hub of heme. If God's
plan for all this function
be heresy, at least let
what came, chanced, to be

be best. Heme, myo- and hemo-
globins, vertebrates' O_2
transport proteins, subunits'
trim fit link—evolved.

4

Carried by blood, carrying
electrons, life-empowering
oxygen. Elsewhere, in engines
it's sucked into carburetor

trains, there to mix with branched
heptanes, octanes, another kind
of feedstock. Sparked, it burns
things in controlled explosions,

a human specialty. And what
thermochemistry says should end
in greening CO_2 and steam, in
incomplete combustion partly

goes to CO, carbon monoxide.
This odorless diatomic tres-
passer sweeps into bronchia, brashly
binding 200 times better

than O_2. A free ride on deoxyhemo-
globin down arteries, right past
cells that long for the other, can't
wait too long before shutdown.

5

So a life ends. That wise blood,
a million years in the making, it
should have fought, that oxygen-
starved blood. But Nature's

a tinkerer, a shanty-town contractor,
filer of misfit gears, the original
found artist. In oxygenated
salty soups, lightning-lit, when

molecules swam to be shaped,
and vines groped for the sun, she
took anything that worked, or the first
that passed the million destructions

of her sweet time lab. No white-
coated intelligences to hurry her
or remind her of the carbon
monoxide that was not there.

This poem owes much to an article by F. Jacob in *Science* (vol. 196, 1161, 1977). Actually there "always" has been some CO there, produced in the body in the course of normal breakdown processes. Hemoglobin and myoglobin bind CO some 100 times less strongly than their component, heme. Presumably the oxygen-carrying mechanism evolved so as to be able to function adequately with the little amount of physiological CO around, and to do that it actually had to *suppress* the CO-binding capability of the heme group. A shaped protein pocket does that. For more on these wondrous proteins see L. Stryer, *Biochemistry*, 3d ed. (New York: W. H. Freeman and Co., 1988), chapter 7.

Stretch Marks

1

It is said in the Talmud that the child in the womb,
flexing her floating sac of the world, knows all, knows
the name of the angel who wrestled with Jacob, knows

and dreams, dreams all molecules her hands will make,
bowties of atoms centered by platinum, carboxypeptidase.
She remembers the constellations' pause as Abraham

held the knife over Isaac, and later, Dachau trains.
Reaching, through her mother's eyes, she blows life
into weeds and carbon chains from comets' tails;

and marks the lust, just that, of her father in her
conception. In volutes of gene threads and shells,
what a time to know! And then . . . a time to be born.

As she is pushed into the colder world, an angel
strikes her on the head, and makes her forget all
she knew inside. The mark of the angel is on our lip.

2

Why does the angel do this? Today they don't announce
themselves, these wheels of God, and, if questioned,
they say: I'm just following orders. Is he Ialdabaoth,

the workman demiurge, who without a host of technicians
and genetic engineering knew, just knew, how to mold
muscle, sheathe a nerve, the nitty-gritty, bone fitting

into bone, of creation? No one's left to believe in him.
So Ialdabaoth, unemployed by this sexy human trick
of procreation, strikes out at children. Or maybe

it's Yahweh, not my Hebrew one Lord, but his dark Gnostic
mask. He keeps men from unhusking the fallen sparks within,
knowing the blue sky that is also the sea of their spirit.

3

Rabbi Baruch of Mezbizh explained it thus: If
the child were not made to forget, she would brood
on her death, the count of years and seconds left

audible like a repeater of death in her mind.
Contemplating her death she would not light candles,
or build a house. So the angel makes her forget.

4

But I think God, who knows, doubts (which is to know)
his design works. His winged observer marks the
onset of contractions, hydraulics of the amniotic

fluid. The angel is drawn into timing, hears
breathing, hoarser, instructed. He touches, an angel's
touch, the dilating neck of the womb. The child's

head is pushed against her own breast, the occiput
leads, rotates into the pelvic floor until bones
won't give, forcing the head to turn, shaping

a conformation that angles up; all this takes time
even if it is not a first birth. As the head emerges,
a thin shoulder slides into the place of resistance;

more pain, a push turning the face into the mother's
thigh. Confronted with this congruence of form and motion,
the angel is the one struck dumb, forgets, must attend

every birth. The mother stirs, unprompted, to the after-
birth; the daughter, like a seal coming up from its deep
dive, depressurizes, gasps for this unforgettable air.

Four

If I Forget You Jerusalem

then let the gold one sun sets
on all old stone be stripped. If
I let the memory of your hills

erode, how would I raise Granada?
Your minarets, Al-Quds, fly me
to storks' nests on blue tile, high

above Bukhara. Friend of an old city,
if I miss the babble at your gates
how will I name the accents of New

York? Dear city, were I to lose sight
of you in snow, would I know Nara,
all towns lightly dusted by snow?

And, if I forget the candelabrum
on Titus's Arch, if I let fade
the jostle of graves down the Mount

of Olives, Yerushalaim, then let
me forget Mycenae, and Nagasaki,
and Warszawa in forty-three and four.

But if I remember? Oh, I do remember!
Then, with the good news of the earth,
the water of spring Gihon, I slip

twelve-hundred cubits down Hezekiah's
curving tunnel, into the pool of Siloam.
Cypress roots reach for this sweet

instruction issuing from Zion. But I,
I grow cold, for I remember more:
The terraced escarpment of David's

city, like the prow of a beached ark
of God, blocks the pool from seeing
(but it also remembers, it was there)

the ruined temple. What ruin? Not
a stone, not a stone upon stone . . .
Elsewhere, archaeologists sift layers

of ash, shards, chips of wall under
wall, razed earthworks, the bottomless
rubble of wars Jerusalem can't forget.

Bora; Bora-Bora

In the myths the islands are pieces of Taaroa's shell. The lone only one, of all things, made a shell, sat in it. Then he broke the shell, which fell into islands. Taaroa called out, there was no answer.

But geologists say the islands rose. The earth heaved, and took its time to build mounds 30,000 ft. from the ocean floor. How it must have boiled!

Rats, birds—no snakes or monkeys. Only what stowed away.

At the reef edge the current is in; a rude shelf growth, above which roils in a foot of water. Then a big wave, flooding the snorkel, saltwater that I have to swallow before I can think to blow the air tube clear. Behind the live reef, there is debris of coral, bleached shells piling up, hermit crabs at home. And when it quiets down, a moray eel glares out of his crevice.

The old man from Delaware is just finishing eight months here. He's been coming since the war: We called it Bobcat Island. One time when I was back, the rats ate the biscuits right off the next bed, using me as a stepping stone: I caught fifteen of the fat buggers.

Crabs scuttling sideways into their holes. Or, on a muddy flat, lined up still, a salute of one red claw up, waiting for our bicycles to pass.

Taught me all the shades between dark blue and green. Taught dappled turquoise, and yellow sand underwater.

How long are you here? Are you long here? Depends what you call long. Thirteen years, the German woman says.

In the forests, rusting 7" guns. Only a few, oldtimers, know the way. The paths are overgrown: We once had a 5" water pipe over the hill to Faanui, but they didn't like it, they took it down.

Around another bend—ahead, the high ridge reaches for shore. Following it down, we see a crook, a clearing in lush green, in the soft and unpassable. Looking up to the mountain, quiet out to sea, stands a scholar's hut in a Sung scroll. We cycle by, and don't see any road leading up to it.

The brightest colors are the *Tridacna* clams studding the dull coral, stuck, flashing succulent lips of algae, the symbiotic colorer, perfect, nervous lip-ice of blue, fuchsia, spotted beige with a wavy green edge.

Coconut trees bent into the wind. Piles of coconuts. Signs saying tabu. The dried husks sell for fuel at 35 cents a pound.

Grapefruit sweet with the taste of lime.

The perfect cheese omelette. The chef says do you like it? Yes. I ask, was it with local cheese. Oh no, Gruyère from France, but the secret, do you want to know it, is crème fraîche in the omelette. It comes from Tahiti once a week.

Picasso fish, *Rhinecanthus aculeatus*, defend, snapping, their coral chapels. They can bite the spines off a sea urchin one by one, then turn the animal over, then eat it.

Steering by the island, in the distance, thin clouds hug the reef line, waiting for darkness's cooling permission to cross; rush in, rain.

Rain passes.

We had to hang up our socks, or the little buggers would take them into their holes. Then you'd find them a few days later, chewed up, that crab smell.

When the wind dies, the lagoon's changes on turquoise reach out, mirroring, to the reef edge, a white fringing quiet.

But when the waves and wind rise in the dark, the crash reaches back for us. It is unseen, damped, easily mistaken for thunder. For what light blinks out there?

Denizen

Coral outcrops; in them moored *Tridacna* clams
flex fleshy purple or green mantles when shaded,
an empress angelfish darts off—reef reflexes
meet the finned intruder in this underwater

Gaudi cathedral. But a few kicks along, the sand
angles down, now lightly dappled by wavelets'
higher tease of sun. The lagoon floor that was
a crater swoops to the murk below. From which

a slow looping looms, white flashing on black.
Ten feet wing tip to fleshy wing tip, rippling
to a soft snap in beat with the swing, in endless
back somersaults, scaleless, shark-leathery

Manta alfredi, weird batoid angel of some deep,
flexing cephalic fins sweeps water, water full
of small lives into its latticed box of a mouth.
Colors and coral fade . . . I remember: Plisetskaya's

Black Swan skim backward, into the void of Bolshoi's
deep stage; satellites' autonomous light on dark
pavane; I see—the slow motion replay of a full
gainer off the high board. I am—a runway,

a black cargo plane forcing a landing on me. I am
the updraft, the raptor, I see claws. But that is air,
and here the devil ray's ring dive magic tows me
out to currents I can't fight. The release,

a roiling brake, comes just before envelopment.
The manta breaks for the surface. In the stretched
moment I see, eel-like, the remora, flat oval
sucking disk stuck to the manta's white underbelly.

Opening a Drawer

This shirt was folded by you, I know
because there is no one else, because
no matter how many times you showed me
I can't get the second fold, back,
right, so that the sleeve runs parallel
to the buttons, and I mangle the small
tuck at the bottom that makes the shirt
fit my drawer, exactly. I'm sure
it's your hands that do it; I think of you,
far away, folding big things, the sheets
we slept on, in another time folding little
baby shirts fastened by real ties. The babies
are grown, the small shirts on others'
(maybe we saved a few in a box in the garage).
But your hands enveloping a child, smoothing
the wrap around a bowl of leftovers . . .
These images come easily, the way you do up
my body. They are my mind's stretch marks, dear.

Christmas, or Was It a Birthday

One odd, light packet is left. Others held
marzipan pigs, some scented soap, a tie
traversed by small camels (that from a wish
list). Gifts from the small people in our life,
pushed shyly into reach, but with fever in
the eye. The felt-tip marker label says
"Pappa this is for you I hope you like
my gift." Praise just feeds on this longing,
primps. She's ready to hug this child. But I,
who never learned to loose her naturally,
examine the packet's folds and taped
bulges, unwrap one layer of crêpe, shake,
say it is definitely not something
to eat. The silk paper then rips to show
the polyurethane pencil-holder—
holes punched for pencils, sized for markers,
even a neat slit for a letter opener.
Held in place by tacks, a paisley fabric
apron hides the plastic. I couldn't praise
it enough then, but it still sits on my desk.

Height

The man
who said
when you're on top
of a mountain
you can't see it
was a miner.

Caldo

For Alberta Cifolelli

There are steep trails into
the hills, but in this land-
scape of the mind no path
is cut for the eye. The way in
is through color, catching
warm round-crowned trees mid-
ground; then I'm let loose on a high
precise horizon that exacts
scanning across for detail
of light on slopes. The shade
of sky provokes a forward
jump to pick up a purple
mass of trees that reach up,
again. To ask if these colors
are, is to touch the land.

But then you've said that
this is more about paint
than grass, or hills; the
fields of water or pasture
remembering the way the air-
brush drove paint, the soft
tree line on the horizon
alive on small flowing
at the edges. The colors,
sharp, abutting, owe much
to quickly drying acrylic.
What I'm jealous of is that
you will feel differently.
Just because you painted it!
You and the paint put time,
like music, in, uneven tempos

struck by the brush passing
to build up land from nothing,
cut a fence, move that bush
four times. I have to make do
with clues of historicity,
a couple of broad strokes
across the hottest tree, or,
my favorite meander calligraphy
in your striated evening sky.

In the Way of Speaking

The man began to climb just as the sun rose, and the starlings' scat song was for him, alone. He picked up a stick to swat grass leaning into the trail, at every thistle crown. His boots grew wet. He was bent down over a beetle when she came down the hill. They laughed, the early walkers. He said something about wanting to reach the top before the sun rose. She said it won't be today, you'd have to get up earlier. He thought about both of them standing together at a fence, slowed to speak by the yellowing light on a roan. But what he said was that he was sorry, he was out of breath, and she replied that she was on the easy downhill part. He remembered coming up early one morning and seeing her dozing on the sofa, poorly covered by a sweater and a newspaper. He had brought her a blanket and covered her and said nothing. Now, on the trail, the man pointed to the horizon and said that he had never seen the sea wrapped around the land so far to the south. Birds flew into the silence. He went up the slope, she down, and when he remembered to glance back she was around the bend. The man climbed higher, stopping to watch a skunk, head down, cross to grub for some food. He thought I'm like that skunk, like the curled poppies. High on the ridge, he lay down on some flat rocks, let the sun warm him. He thought of what he should have said. Perhaps he slept ten minutes. Then he woke suddenly, stood up, stretched his arms to the sky. A few feet away on the stone lay a rattlesnake, its head following his hands. He put them down slowly, said Sister rattler. The snake's skin shone in the sun. I love you, sister rattler. I want your power. The man stood, eyes on the snake, stood still, until the memory of what she had said once about keeping calm and not moving if bitten, so that the venom not circulate, burst into his mind, breaking his and the rattler's space. He jumped from the rock and ran down the trail, not looking back.

Imposing Prospect

For Vivian Torrence

The landscape may be different; here,
in clinging fog, the Santa Cruz hills'
grass tops still fodder-green, over-
lapping, cascade to the sea. Or, there,
in Andalusia, brown rocks that never saw
grass fit for a goat. In resonant heat-
light link to the afternoon sun, the
earth rests so as not to crack more. There.

But here, or there, the instrumented
reconnaissance of the scientist strews
the landscape with numbers. Heat over
the central valley (34.6°C at Fresno
at noon, falling with elevation, 33,
31, 29), inland heat, draws the fog in
offshore. From the top the sun flings
digits of heat to droplets absorbing
the energy that will disperse them.
Spanish ground is cored with numbers;
depths, feldspar gradients across faults.

The hills are quiet, the hills are old.
So our inner, hid, slipping by the metering
glance, sneaks another look at these
dangerous hills, stocks them with life.
There be monsters here, and not just real
rattlesnakes, but rearing wild horses,
a banana slug that turns into bêche-
de-mer, or, saltwater hippos. We try
to fence them in, in the shadowed canyons,
and, with the freedom of dreams, let them
fight each other, lest they lunge at us.

Conduit

Maps instruct that dashed
lines across contours mean tunnels.
A rush, whoosh through,

pressure damping sound,
into green light, the train stretching an arc
of disclosed intent

to reach a somewhere
and doing it, creak by clack. Veering
in from right, on side-

swipe trajectory
a flooded sweep, perhaps an abandoned
track. The water deepens,

green to black, half-
corseted in stone, is someone's
needed canal,

goods traffic or drink.
We can't make out which way it flows. Then
sky fills with a mounting

line. How will that water
shear on rock? In the one bend left
we see a tunnel for

the aqueduct, whose
plane mirrors the tunnel's dark
maw, arch, a holy

approximation
to channel shape; space that was rock,
full-face bored, filled

to hide from flow
a convexity underneath,
to hold dear water

to the air before
rushing-up, but still shadowed
penetration.

Hydropathic

The winter-
matted grass
has strong feelings
about water.
That flatness, lack
of spring,
it owes
to the stolid oppression
of one phase. It's not nice
to keep
in your shape
such cold memory.
Then it rains a spell, and
some newly wet,
not beading,
soaks in. You
find yourself crackling
in the wind,
afraid of drying,
brittling sun.
Can there be too much water?
Not for the empowered,
rooting worms,
not for the straight,
the green,
thirstier,
pushing up from below.

The Social Contract

Part of me is the rain,
falling
because its weight
is unbearable to the air,
falling.

Another part of me
builds shelter,
a hip roof
to keep the rain
that must fall
out.

Then I am the gutter
which has little to do
with protection,
or falling
(though it thinks about falling,
it has a slant).
Gutters are about channeling
and foresight.
They ask to be painted.

However, what I really want to be
is the heavy metal
link chain hanging
from a hole in the gutter.
Water and the chain,
there's real freedom:
flow, to dive, scatter,
skip a few, spatter
blowzy all down

hitting the concrete cylinder
that weights the chain.
That's when I think

about responsibility—
you don't want this chain
whipping around, banging
against the house.

The rain
is now in the drain,
constrained.

I lead it down clay pipes
into the expectant earth,
where I tell it: now
you are water, free
to be drunk by my beetles,
to disperse
down to clay, aquifers.
Then you will be conducted
out
to the air
that will pull on you.
And I will tell both of us
you've gone down far enough.
And I will show myself the way up.

Five

Modes of Representation

If you look in old chemistry books
you see
all those line cuts
of laboratory experiments
in cross-section.
The sign for water
is a containing line, the meniscus
(which rarely curls up the walls of the beaker),
and below it
a sea
of straight horizontal dashes
carefully unaligned vertically.
Every cork or rubber stopper
is cutaway.
You can see inside
every vessel
without reflections, without getting wet,
and explore every kink
in a copper condenser.
Flames are outlined cypresses
or a tulip at dawn,
and some Klee arrows
help to move gases and liquids the right way.
Sometimes a disembodied hand
holds up a flask.
Sometimes there is an unblinking observer's eye.
Around 1920
photoengraving
became economically feasible
and took over.
Seven-story distillation columns
(polished up for the occasion),
like giant clarinets,
rose in every text, along
with heaps of chemicals, eventually in color.
Suddenly

water and glass, all reflection
became difficult.
One had to worry about light,
about the sex
and length of dress or cut of suit
of the person sitting at the controls of this impressive
       instrument.
Car models and hairstyles
dated the books more
than the chemistry in them.
Around that time
teachers noted a deterioration
in the students' ability to follow
a simple experimental procedure.

Organic, Inorganic

For Anna Valentina Murch

I've been watching the planting
outside your window, Anna, the one
Chris worked on for two days. He
surrounded each bush or flower

by a circular earthwork to hold
water; it's wet right now,
but John says this place *is*
about water. If you watch

for a while you spot some lizards
and though I've never seen more
than two at a time, I imagine
there is one in each plant, and

that they crawl between, quickly
crossing the exposed space. So . . .
let's find a flat field (that will
be difficult) covered with the four

grasses that grow here. We'll
remove all the grass from some
roughly circular areas. The ground
will be brown underneath, it

can be raked smooth. A little way
out of each circle the grass
will be cut down a few inches
(this must be done by hand).

In the middle of each clearing
we will build a pyramid of one

of the elements in its natural state:
yellow crystals of sulfur, native

copper, white phosphorus, anthracite
more stable than diamond. Oxygen
will be in a balloon the color
of arterial blood. In the grass

between the circles I see connecting
channels of light, water, radiation,
wind, fire . . . the forces that tear,
tear to build. To be gentle on this land

we could use ribbons, a linked chain
of mirrors, plaited shades of blue
and green, taut violet wires, a strand
of naval flags. These we'll string

low in the grass, so that as you
and I walk through, one or another
ribbon will be seen. And we'll come
back and watch the weeds grow in.

At a Cocktail Party,
the 32d National Meeting of the
American Vacuum Society

First pump down the steel chamber.
The burble is reassuring, you know
something is being removed. But your

conventional high vacuum is not
enough. You need a getter: Shiny
ultra-pure barium wire, made up pretty

in the shape of a ring or stirrup.
Introduce it through a baffle,
with a threaded screw. Watch it

change (there are ports) from metal
to chalky gray. And you thought
there was nothing there! Few materials

have good gettering properties.
Our company makes one to eat up
any volatile loose in your system.

Like a Gas Flame Going Out
with the Sound of Trying for Life

He says:
You know that copper kettle—
before you boil water in it, remember
it needs retinning. There's nothing
wrong with it being unsteady—
the bottom didn't matter then,
it was that fine ring, flaring
that fit over a hole
in the wood stove.

She says:
All the time we were talking
his hands were moving,
brushing away imaginary flies,
pushing the sleeves down over
those blue-gray arms.
Then he'd roll them up again.

He says:
I have this dream
that I'm part of a machine
making some chemical.
Feedstocks come in, a pipe
out of my mouth. One night
there is this dry feeling
that wakes me up,
my mouth is filling up
with a powder.
That wasn't in the plan, but it's a factory
and I guess things go wrong
once in a while.

She says:
I asked him if he wanted more oxygen,

but he said, less,
too much oxygen is not good for you,
remember the Mercury astronauts.
I told him I'd bring the children
next time.

He says:
I remember
the view of Toledo
from across the Tagus. And this madonna
holding twins in her arms.

She says:
At the end he just kept talking
about this woman
leading him, holding him
the way a man does,
dancing the tango.

What We Have Learned about the Pineal

Descartes just knew, being, knew
that so central an organ confined
mechanism and mind, entwined.

So people studied it. But the gland
refused to be of use, except to lizards
who, when they lost it (Descartes

liked dissection) couldn't change skin
tint. In humans it calcifies after puberty
to a neat X-ray beacon. That's all

we could do with this small centrality
until Aaron Lerner, digesting kilos
of bovine pineals, isolated melatonin,

N-acetyl-5-methoxytryptamine, a mine
of a name. The hormone did change
the color of tadpoles. In the tuotara,

a New Zealand lizard, in lampreys,
the gland rises from the brain on a stalk,
an eye-like structure, a third

unblinking eye just below the skin.
Our pineal is not photosensitive.
It synthesizes melatonin all the time

but more in the dark, so a diurnal rhyme,
seasons timed in melatonin levels.
Some depressions are helped by bright

light . . . In hamsters melatonin sets sex
cycles, but Josephine Arendt tells us
that "given to humans at a time of day

(late afternoon) calculated to maximize
sexually related effects" it makes
us sleepy. So not the seat of the soul,

but still a gland to reckon with, a gland
to tell time. Descartes died of a fever
in Christina's sunless February Sweden.

Some of the material in this poem derives from an article by Josephine Arendt in
New Scientist, 25 July 1985, p. 36.

In Need of Mending

A fence keeps the outside out;
for instance, if this a neat
house and there be cattle, we don't
want the cows to do away with
seven years of landscaping by
letting them in where they shouldn't
be. They leave cow-pies all over.
And think about new ideas!

The fence also keeps the inside
in. This is not very important,
unless you have small children
or German shepherds. But then
one day you fly into Berlin
and see a hundred meters of cleared
earth, a wall, you feel the mines
there, waiting . . . And how would it
be if I told you I said something
stupid, or asked to be forgiven?

But now things get complicated.
The fence I see has stakes or
slats, so the fixity of intent
of the one to keep outside out or
inside in is undercut by this in-
sistence on letting in out (or out in).

And suppose the fence goes around
your friend's field too, so that you
two share a stretch, which may be
long. Then it becomes very confusing.
Part of your outside is someone
else's inside; and, what's worse,
it's even true the other way around!
There's more; those outside the two

of you see one single fence around,
not caring that you tend the part.

I'll tell you some fences I like:
membranes, assemblies of proteins
and lipids that define the outer
wall of cells, then fold into in-
finitely crenelated surface. Mem-
branes that bound organelles, the double
membranes of nuclei and mitochondria;
flexible molecular fences, replete
with gates, pumps, stylish chemical
conduits, responding to dim light,
firing neurons. It seems that in
this life, to sequester is to free.

And I love: balustrades, because
they bound passages up or down,
because they hint of balconies,
ballrooms and terraces, and the word,
what a word, sings of the calyx
of a flower of a wild pomegranate.

Altitudes Change Attitudes

When we first see them
we scan quickly, up,
so that the heart not
miss, so that they be,
and not the mushroom
cloud. Air traffic skirts

thunderheads, until
hemmed in by three
megacephalic white
risers we yield, enter
the empire of clouds.
Here small wisps,

condensates reign,
in calm belied
by the plane's bob.
We know air is
a fluid, but who
is skipping us across

this surface? At times
like these, it's soothing
to think of Avogadro's
number of molecules
colliding, set on
a random jig by heat

and the absence of it
exchanged where cliffs
and sea chance to meet.
Sucked about by lows,
whirling—nothing
definite, aimed at us

could come from such
sweet and airy chaos?
Sure enough—a break,
(how nice now to fly)
a glimpse of a bed-
scape for outsize

gods, flash-frozen
billows, a nesting
peace that might come
from falling, unarrested.
Now the fleece moves,
rushes up. Wings slice

into gray, again. The
clouds have kept the sun
for their own purposes. We
drop, precipitously.
In the empire of clouds
the dark one rains.

Thèse pour Obtenir le Grade de Docteur ès-Sciences

On this gray afternoon
the lights are off, a European habit.
Aquiline features against a
blackboard of meandering equations,
Besançon defends his thesis.

Constrained to a line,
tied by springs
two molecules collide—
in resonant motion,
most certain phase, united.

Hands behind back,
one grasping the other,
it helps to exercise control . . .
and exorcise fear.
Gray suit, neat shirt, but no tie.
In protest against the establishment
Besançon defends his thesis.

Equations of motion
simulate the quantum mechanical
reality of a reaction.
Resonances, branch points
orchestrate a dynamic model.

The audience, restive,
undulates in stochastic fashion.
I flex a muscle,
shift to catch sight
of a bared calf.
The seat sticks to my pants.
Besançon defends his thesis.

The jury of five poses questions
good, bad, indifferent.
Each congratulates the finesse,
the pondering of difficulties.
Besançon drones on in reply,
multiplexing the simplicity of a question.
My French fades in and out
on a sleepy Clermont-Ferrand afternoon.

Be Wanting

In this lab you may see women studying
failure. Not of crosswalks in hotel atriums,
not the Russian harvest, but the mind

route of failure, the ken and feel of coming
up short, against, hard into. The not
of things. Women are well-suited for failure

research: shuttle missions abort, what
miscarriages of justice, they labored
in vain to revive Natasha, and this term

tax reform was a stillborn idea. Women
are at home with failure: husbands' egos
and surrogates must be appropriately

stroked, for he can't go off to work
depressed. Their talk is never sparkling
enough, and they bring up snapped clutch

cables when all a man wants is to watch
the Giants score. So these women with high
degrees have hypnotized the man who could

have screamed a warning to the girl, tape
electrodes to a Georgian weight lifter straining
to jerk ten pounds over his best. Natasha

safe, the weight up . . . there, these *were*,
harpoons of soul intent. Maybe the lines
just got a bit snarled. With a feint

on the what might have been, with a soft
touch, it could be set right. They are encouraged
to hear that physicists, men, now think

seriously of shadow worlds. The women
pick one of their own, still young and good
at math, to study knit lifeline topologies.

Somewhere

In me are hidden constellations.

Once I managed to sight one
through a lens of equations
that could be solved only
approximately. Still,
with that imperfect rule
I taught others the electrons'
lobed motions. I'm wrong, often,
I work this wild chemical
garden with one old tool.

Let me show others new ways to see.

In me is the word that slaps worlds into being.

I muffled the word, but now
I let it sing a little,
watch owls and turkey
vultures. I try to teach
the word of mitochondria
as vestigial symbiotes;
it sulks, promises to sing
of both worlds if I let it
fly. But what binds it, binds me.

Free the word, world in me.

In me is a buried river that washes the mother lode.

Early on, an earthquake
covered it. The river

shifted, then filled
in with detritus, gravel,
the silt of slow seasonal
motions. An occasional
nugget washes to the surface.

Sink a shaft to touch me, love.

Six

Eschatology

I once attended a scientific meeting
in Maynooth, the Pontifical Seminary of Ireland.
The invited speakers
were given the bishops' rooms, while
the others attending
stayed where the seminarians lived.
The difference was
that the bishops' rooms
were twice as large,
had two fireplaces
to be stoked with peat briquets, stacked
like brown egg-cartons
in the hall.
And hard to light.
It was an Irish April,
I had to pile more briquets on the fires
twice each night.
I had always wanted to see a bishop's bathroom.
Ireland probably has a lot of bishops,
because we had this whole floor
and a large communal bathroom.
It was dark, a kind of labyrinth of marble partitions
ending at eye level,
shower heads sticking up above,
like gray metallic sunflowers.
So you could see your fellow bishops
standing up,
but not sitting down.
The labyrinth was made of cubicles,
each with a door to a bath and a toilet.
Some of the doors were missing.
I went into one cubicle, looked
if there were a hook for the bishop
to hang up his cassock.
I tried to imagine
the sound
of the pastors of Ireland passing water.

Grand Unification

This is just a rule; strings that meet,
wriggling in their roughened-up space-time,
if their tips just touch, they must merge,

and bigger lines, loops, necklaces or thatchings
self-assemble. This is so. But it is not real,
it's just a rule. Loops tangle, there is an exchange

of quantum numbers, the stray collision
sets the strings rotating, rippling, a whip
and then the extra snap looses a particle

(boson or fermion) and light, any color. The math
says it must be so. Mind you, this is not: people,
passing, a look that locks on some missed braid

of a future. This is not: a hummingbird's tie
to the sweet and red, tie testing stasis.
And it is not the interlace of frost, another

season's nonlinear history of steam meanders.
Nor: rope dancers . . . For those you need words.
But here just watch the math, follow it across

or around or down, just follow its unhusking
to the small world, where intuition is strung
out as far as it will give, but equations

work as well here as for real billiard balls,
whirling dervishes or galaxies (there is no need
for me to say all this). In this smallness infinities,

anomalies slough off, the loops vibrate, a keen
undulation, clockwise rippling nothingness
in ten dimensions. Twenty-six the other way.

This fits. But it's not all. The dimensions
must compactify, in a silent crumpling, curling
in of what there's room for, into inwards' innards.

The quantum numbers then come out naturally,
strung out on a loop that is gravity, the source
of all interactions. We are *so* near understanding

everything. I believe, reasons without words,
classy symmetries. It's a rule. And up scale the sun
shines, frost melts and zing! go the strings of my heart.

The Man for Whom Everything Came Easy

came from an immigrant family
and didn't own a book
until he was 16.
So his first desires were simple:
Fournier playing the Bach cello sonatas, an illuminated globe.
Since he did well in school,
and this was America,
it was easy.
He worked hard,
did interesting research
and in time he could buy
a Nikon with two telephoto lenses
and a second recording of the Bach sonatas
(he had made a mistake about Fournier).
He was a little unhappy
that when they needed a new second car
his wife said that his joking suggestion of a Porsche
just didn't make sense.
Invitations to speak came from all over the world.
What he wanted most (but this he was afraid to say)
was that his children read good books,
and not waste their time on hard rock.
This was more difficult to arrange,
because you couldn't pay your children
to do what they didn't like to do. But in time
they grew up, picked up Tolstoy
and even, once in a while,
put the cello sonatas on the record player.
The man who seemed to do everything well
actually began to like rock
at least to dance to it
(he still complained that he couldn't hear the lyrics).
Running six miles each day,

he had less trouble than his wife in keeping his weight down.
He began to fly first class,
and sat in on a class on Kierkegaard.
The man who had everything
now told his new intellectual friends:
What I would really like is to have my soul
as it is not.

Carcinoma

This old anatomical drawing
shows a front and back view
of a man's lymphatic system.
Nodes are dark numbered circles, lines
connect the nodes.
You have cut out these two views into triangles,
and mounted them,
tête-bêche, like a Jack of Hearts,
except that where the hearts should be
you've painted in a pair of dice.
The card is above a body of dashed-line water.
To the left,
on a hummocked shore,
there appear to be several artillery batteries,
soldiers in black and white outlined Hussar dress.
One group is passing balls to be loaded.
In another, the powder fuse is lit by a bearded officer.
Some green grass has been painted in, and
you have drawn the trajectory
of a shot from one of these cannons
towards the card.
But it's going to fall short.
At top right, in a dark sky
there is a loupe projecting, as if
someone big, prismatic
were watching this scene.
The card is held above water by a woman.
She seems to be struggling in the sea,
though she holds the card steady.
She's small,
and it looks like you've Xeroxed an old passport photo of yourself
and used it as her face.
There is a dot of red,
the only warm color in this collage,
where one might imagine her heart would be.

Terrorists

In the dark that is the bed,
in the dark, that is the sole
room in this life, we seem

to be taming a cat. The woman
with me is wife, or mother,
or both, and we are intent

on this impossible task of
training an animal we can't
see. We do hear it, its pacing,

always out of reach, and when
it jumps (this we have learned
to fear most, the silent space

of its jump) it lands claws out,
with the smooth unthinking cat
cut of claw into skin and flesh.

The sheets are twisted, they will
be bloody in the morning. Lately
it seems to be timing its jumps.

The woman and I are not sure
who in this night of training,
will be taught to kill whom.

Longing

The earth births shapes
in the mind that no real

land or laboratory knew:
what a fissure might divulge,

dry rocks askew, the way
a mesa waits for first

light. To free me of these
forms I sculpt mockups

of wire, burlap, clay.
When they dry, brown and

rough in parts, I walk around
them with my hands and then

I draw them. Why do they
always make me think of you?

Corral

For Carlos Fuentes

1

To grow animal, smart, the membranes
of eucaryotic cells rim, twice, the
coded library of the nucleus, tangle

then fuse to the gaudy network of sacs
of the endoplasmic reticulum. Pinched off
subcellular organelles empower cells

with the know-how to reject transplants,
wrap a myelin sheath around a neuron, see
red, and then, see yellow. Still better

microscopes make out more partitions.
In the emerging inner texture, freedom,
to change, is built from lipid-tailored

confinements, warm prisons where enzyme
brews gel. Ways in and out are ingenious:
shaped pores, embrasures, and this chemical

escalator called active transport. Fluid,
mosaic, the membranes' holed sequestering works.

2

In 1655 Juana Inés de Asbaje begged
her mother to dress her as a boy, so
that she could study at the University

of Mexico. At the court of the viceroy
she astounded forty professors with her
mathematics and Latin odes. But it was not

a time for learned women in Mexico, so
Juana entered the convent of San Jerónimo;
within, watched two girls spinning a top, and

from what she called her black inclination
for wisdom, had flour sprinkled, so that as
the top danced out its loss of momentum

one might see its spiral trace, and not
a circle. Juana mixed earths, and in a library
of 4,000 volumes wrote theology and love

poems. Sor Juana Inés de la Cruz, shutting
herself in the cell where knowing is permitted.

About the Author

Roald Hoffmann was born in 1937 in Złoczów, then Poland, now the Soviet Union. After surviving the Nazi occupation and after several years of postwar wandering in Europe, he and his mother and stepfather made their way to the United States in 1949, settling in New York City. He graduated from Stuyvesant High School, Columbia University, and from Harvard University with an M.A. in physics and Ph.D. in chemical physics. Since 1965, Hoffmann has been engaged in teaching and research in theoretical chemistry at Cornell University, where he is now John A. Newman Professor of Physical Science.

Hoffmann's research interests are wide-ranging and his work has earned him numerous honors and awards, including the 1981 Nobel Prize in Chemistry, which he shared with Kenichi Fukui. Hoffmann is interested in the geometry and reactivity of molecules, in explaining from calculations of the motions of molecules' electrons why those molecules have the structures they do and why they react in specific ways. He likes to characterize as "applied theoretical chemistry" the particular blend of computations generated by experiment with the construction of generalized models that is his contribution to chemistry.

Hoffmann had his first real introduction to poetry at Columbia from Mark Van Doren, the great teacher and critic whose influence was at its height in the 1950s. Through the years Hoffmann has maintained his interest in literature, particularly German and Russian literature. He began to write poetry fourteen years ago, but it was only in 1984 that his work began to be published. Hoffmann owes much to a poetry group at Cornell that includes A.R. Ammons, Phyllis Janowitz, and David Burak, and to Maxine Kumin.

Hoffmann also writes essays on science, literature, and art. In 1990 he will appear on PBS presenting a series called "The World of Chemistry."

University of Central Florida
Contemporary Poetry Series